Inside OUT

RELATING GARDEN TO HOUSE

Page Dickey

PHOTOGRAPHS BY
Richard Felber

STEWART, TABORI & CHANG | NEW YORK

Project editor: Sandra Gilbert

Designer: Susi Oberhelman

Production: Pamela Schechter

Published in 2000 by

Stewart, Tabori & Chang

A division of U.S. Media Holdings, Inc.

115 West 18th Street

New York, NY 10011

Distributed in Canada by

General Publishing

30 Lesmill Road

Don Mills, Ontario, Canada M3B 2T6

Library of Congress Cataloging-in-Publication Data

Dickey, Page.

Inside out : relating garden to house / Page Dickey ; photographs by Richard Felber.

p. cm.

ISBN 1-58479-046-6

1. Gardens—United States—Design. 2. Garden rooms—United States.

I. Title.

SB473 .D48 2000

712'.6'0973—dc21   00-041296

Printed in Italy

First Printing

10 9 8 7 6 5 4 3 2 1

FOR BOSCO

Contents

Introduction

The doors from the original entrance, kitchen, and porch of my nineteenth-century farmhouse determined the siting of the small hedged-in gardens around it. Like so many old houses, the front door now is rarely used except to enter the garden; instead we come and go through the porch, right, which opens onto a little courtyard. Here, four 'Snowdrift' crab apples are planted formally in box-edged beds.

A FEW YEARS AGO, after a talk I gave in California, a young woman in the audience asked me what I would advise her to do first when starting a garden. I urged her to stand at the doors leading out of her house, look out her windows, and start plotting her garden from those vantage points. I suggested that she think about paths, about views, axes, and perspectives. Consider the idea of outdoor rooms extending from the house, rooms created with frames in the form of hedges, fences, or walls, that might partially conceal one part of the garden from another, afford-

ing an element of surprise. A central axis or winding path leading from the house through these garden rooms would lure you out on an adventure.

I also suggested that my young friend keep in mind the style of garden that would be most appropriate for her house and its setting. The deep woods of northern New England suggest a different sort of garden than one suited to the dry, baking hot climate of California. When choosing plants, I advised her to take the old vernacular plantings of her area and the surrounding indigenous landscape as her guide. And because the garden is to be closely connected to the home, keep its outline and personality in harmony with the building's architecture. A geometric or formally structured garden might best echo the feel of a traditional house with symmetrical details, while a modern home might cry out for wild, free-form beds.

Now, all this advice is easy for me to offer after three decades of learning from the mistakes I made in my gardens, gleefully digging those first years with absolutely no advance thought or consciousness of design.

I know now that, ideally, a close relationship exists between a house and its garden,

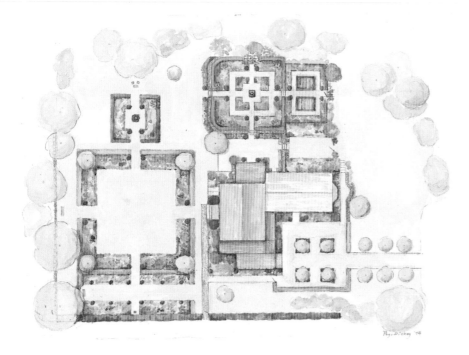

a physical connection as well as a marriage of style and atmosphere. But most of us start out plotting a garden in a void, thinking only of the pleasure of growing some lettuces and tomatoes or a border of gaudy flowers. My first garden, if you could call it that, was a row of flowers along the boundary fence. My second garden was plunked down in the middle of my backyard in a patch of sun, and it gave me, simply, enormous satisfaction. I didn't care, I wasn't even aware, that it couldn't be seen from the house, that it was awkward to get to, that it had no visual connection to the house whatsoever. You went out the back door, diagonally across the lawn, over the driveway, sideways down a treacherous slope, and stumbled upon it.

I had always been interested in plants. At first I devoured books on perennials, bulbs, wildflowers, roses, wanting to know their habits and culture. But eventually I began reading books on garden design, classics like *The Education of a Gardener*, by Russell Page, and, closer to home, the writings of New Yorkers Helen Fox and Louise Beebe Wilder. I studied garden plans in *America's Garden Book* by Bush-Brown, and the diaries of our country's outstanding early-twentieth-century landscape gardener, Beatrix Farrand.

The lessons I learned in those books came alive for me in a garden I owned for five years, which had been skillfully laid out

by a landscape architect at the turn of the century. The driveway ran through a woodland of oak and dogwood and circled around to the long north side of the house where the entrance and kitchen were located. The south side opened onto the garden through French doors all along its length. Because the land sloped away from the house, the Edwardian landscaper designed two grass terraces, divided by stone retaining walls and broad steps. To add grace and light shade, he planted crab apple trees on both terraces,

The kitchen opens onto a small gravel terrace and a barberry-hedged herb garden. From a bench underneath an arbor smothered with honeysuckle and ramblers, you look back past the sundial to the kitchen's French doors.

and then laid out flower borders along the walls. On the lower terrace, a yew hedge divided this formal part of the garden from the natural landscape beyond; glimpses of meadow could be seen through its openings, where more steps led down and out into the wildness. I reveled in the way the garden seemed to flow from the house, graciously leading you down into the landscape, and reveled, too, in the views from inside. Living in that house, I came to the full realization that a garden is most satisfying when it is wedded to the house it surrounds.

When I moved again, nineteen years ago, I went from having an established, mature garden with superb bones to having none at all. No gardens, no terraces, no paths or steps, no hedges or fences surrounded my new home. I had virtually a clean slate. Miserable without a garden, I set off immediately to put what I'd learned to use.

The prim old farmhouse seemed an obvious jumping off point for the small garden areas that have evolved around it. Drawing on graph paper at first, and staking out my ideas with bamboo and mason's twine, I planned axes from its various doors, working my way outside in uncomplicated geometric patterns to form hedged-in areas of trees and flowers. Eventually, each area, or room, had a different emphasis (on herbs or shrub roses or shade-loving perennials) and a separate color scheme. The classic symmetry and simplicity of the house suggested a garden formal in outline but filled with an unpretentious jumble of old-fashioned plants.

Now, every morning in summer, I slip out the unused front door of the house in my bathrobe and slippers to walk in the square

The porch is my indoor garden in winter, and pleasant to enter on bitter cold days when the forced daffodils, hyacinths, and crocuses are blooming.

garden of flowers and crab apples centered on its axis. The kitchen, where, it seems, I spend much of my day, opens out through French doors onto a terrace spilling with herbs. The porch door, which is the most used entrance to the house from the parking area, leads past four boxwood-edged beds of white-flowering crabs underplanted with early white daffodils and myrtle. Upstairs, the windows of bedrooms and bathrooms look down on all sides to patterns of gardens.

Because I love fragrance, I chose sweet-scented shrubs and flowers as well as pungent herbs whenever possible, especially where their perfume might waft in through the doors and windows, or be brushed against as you walk down a path from the house. Low daphnes, like *D.* x *burkwoodii* and *D. caucasica*, scent my ground floor bedroom on a warm May day. The 'Miss Kim' lilac (*Syringa patula*) on the kitchen terrace is heady with perfume in early June. The pungent leaves of bayberries can be rubbed and smelled on the walk to the barn all year long. Winter honeysuckle (*Lonicera fragrantissima*) throws lemony perfume in the air for at least a month in earliest spring.

Mine is a rather traditional example of a garden closely connected to its house. What is fun and exciting about gardening in America is that it holds infinite possibilities.

Our landscapes are so varied, our regional climates so rich in extremes, and our architecture so diverse, that our gardens and homes can have wildly different characters. This book describes a sampling of these personal American gardens created with imagination, charm, and artistry as intimate extensions of the houses they surround. ▪

In the courtyard outside, the graceful crabs and boxwood squares are as appealing to the eye in winter as they are in spring.

"THIS WAS ORIGINALLY just a week-end house, no maintenance, the house of knotty pine," Lee Link says with amusement, surveying her transformed bungalow perched high on a hill in the lush, rolling landscape of northwestern Connecticut. Over the last twenty years, Lee has been busy embellishing the simple weathered A-frame structure, adding architectural details as well as major extensions that now house summer porches, a plant-filled conservatory, and guest quarters, all lapped by intimate terraces and gardens. With her innate sense of style, she has created such a beguiling nest, one that is so comfortable and pleasing to the eye, and that so deliciously embraces the outdoors, it is difficult not to want to linger long after the weekend has ended.

Lee and her husband Fritz decided to look for a country place of their own in 1980 after renting a house in this same idyllic New England town five years in a row. "We wanted an old house but we couldn't afford to fix it up. We needed a house intact. When we saw this place, I said to Fritz, it's very different than how we live in the city." And that appealed. In New York City, the Links had a traditional apartment, with separate rooms for dining and living. This house was all muddled together, with the kitchen cozily in the living room. They bought it and moved in. At

Porches in the Summer Garden

Lee Link's Solution for Indoor-Outdoor Living

first they didn't do much. "It was a stretch for us," Lee recalls; "we had to wait and reload."

In a way, Lee says, it was nice that the house was so bland when they bought it. "We could make it into anything we wanted." Gradually she changed the look of the 1960s façade, projecting the peeked roof line out several inches to give it a more three-dimensional feel, adding a birdhouse

Lee Link transformed an A-frame bungalow by projecting the roof line, putting mullions in the windows, and adding screened porches to open the house to the outdoors. Informal terraces and flower borders outside the doors meld into the soft rolling landscape of fields and woodland.

15

A breezeway off the master bedroom was turned into a summer sleeping porch. It is tucked beneath the living room on a terraced level of the hillside, affording views outdoors of garden and countryside. Climbing hydrangea flourishes by the doorway, and a weathered teak bench sits beneath a walled border of Russian sage (*Perovskia atriplicifolia*) and wine-colored drumstick alliums.

at the top, and changing all the windows to ones with mullions. "Mullions frame things," Lee observes, "they cozy up the place." Then Lee extended the house front to jut out three feet beneath the living room-kitchen, enlarging a breezeway just off the master bedroom on the ground floor. She enclosed the new room with screens on three sides (and storm windows in the wintertime) to make a sleeping porch. Here she sleeps in summer on a plump settee made from tree trunks that affords a view of gardens and fields all around. The sleeping porch is also Lee's garden room, where her tools stand ready and her garden books pile up. On the

arm of an old wicker chair, clippers and a hand pruning saw lie waiting to be grabbed, gardening boots and shoes share the stone floor with old wooden birdhouses and wicker cutting baskets. A great tin pot in one corner holds a pickaxe, brooms, a garden fork, and stakes, which in turn support her straw hats.

Just outside the sleeping porch is "my own shower and hot tub," Lee says with the satisfaction of someone who knows she's found a bit of paradise. The hot tub is sunken in a stone-walled terrace at the end of a long wooden pergola that connects the house with what was once the garage but is now a charming guesthouse. "I will only have a wood hot tub," Lee states with conviction, admitting, however, that it does leak every once in a while. "That's the pure way. And it has to be very close to the house or I wouldn't use it at night. I like to go just before bed when the fireflies are out, or after gardening. You just get that jet on the lower back area and say, 'Oh yes, thank you God!'"

From the shade of the wisteria-twined pergola or submerged in the hot tub, you have a pastoral view of meadows and soft wooded hills in the distance, and, closer at hand, sidelong glimpses of the flower borders that extend along the front of the house. The stretch of border running along the stone retaining wall just below the sleeping porch and pergola, Lee calls the cutting gar-

den. Delicate flower stalks of a tall yellow mustard, grown by Lee from seed, billow beside blue salvias and variegated plectranthus. Flame honeysuckle, morning glories, passion flowers, and scarlet canary vine climb wispily up a series of slender steel trellises between stands of red dahlias and clumps of sunflowers. Three standard dwarf Korean lilacs, clipped hard to a stout umbrella shape, were the first thing Lee put in the border to give it some structure. "They've done really

Left: A wisteria-draped pergola, made of wooden beams and roping, connects Lee's sleeping porch with the guest cottage (formally the garage). **Above:** A wooden hot tub at the end of the pergola is a good vantage point for viewing the cutting garden along the stone retaining wall, and the distant pastoral landscape.

well; now you have to get a little mean with them," she says. Lee added wattle fencing to the border this past year to give it more pattern, more definition. The low wattle weaves through the bed creating enclosed spaces where lettuces and leeks, nasturtiums, snapdragons, and nicotiana are planted in blocks. "Before, it was a smudge."

Seven years ago, with the help of her contractor, Stan Dzneutis, Lee designed the summer porch—a twenty-five foot by fifteen foot wing extending out from the small, cozy kitchen-living area. "It was my first building project," she says, describing how she poured over books and magazines for inspiration. "I

started out with a much smaller screened porch, and then I thought, 'I don't think it could be too big'; then I went outside to see how it would look in proportion to the house. The first size would have been dinky." The resulting addition, amply proportioned and built of the same wood as the rest of the house, looks as if it has always been there. Enclosed on three sides with screen from floor to ceiling, similar to the sleeping porch but on a grander scale, the room holds a long glass-and-wrought-iron dining table surrounded by slipcovered chairs, an Empire daybed piled with pillows, a chaise lounge, and comfortably-cushioned old wicker chairs.

Off the living room and kitchen, Lee added a twenty-five-by-fifteen-foot screened porch, (protection against northwestern Connecticut's bugginess), where she and her husband spend much of their time in the summer. By attaching the short side of the porch to the house, rather than the more traditional long side, and using screening between every bracket and support, the room seems to float out into the garden.

Books and magazines lie around enticingly, and pots of flowers—pansies, fuchsias, and pineapple lilies (*Eucomis*) in September—mingle with bibelots. "We live here in the summer," Lee says.

The shorter end of the porch butts the house causing the length of the porch to jut out "so you're really floating." In a brilliant stroke, she had the carpenter use screening, rather than a solid piece of wood, for the triangular peak at the end of the porch. The result is a wonderfully airy room, barely a room at all but for its inviting furnishings, just gauze between you and the outdoors.

The back of the summer porch looks out onto a small stone terrace, a stretch of lawn, and a shady garden of hostas and ferns at the foot of what Lee describes as "a mountain of ledge rock." The house indeed

backs up against a dramatically rocky, wooded slope. Lee stopped by a local nursery going out of business and asked to buy some hosta. The owner said if she took them all he'd sell them for two dollars a piece. She accepted the deal, got a truck, brought them home, "and that was the beginning of the shade garden." For some reason—perhaps, Lee thinks, because of this formidable hillside of rock behind the house—they have no trouble with deer eating their plants.

Steps made of bluestone set on edge between grass treads curve from the porch door down past stone retaining walls to the big flower border below. Here Lee has planted a bold mixed border, ten feet deep, of large-growing shrubs, perennials and annuals in strong colors—yellows, purple, garnet red, chartreuse—'Black Knight' buddleia, *Nicotiana sylvestris*, angelica, black hollyhocks, *Artemisia lactiflora*, *Thalictrum rochenbrunianum*. These she mixes with the dusky plum foliage of purple smokebush, *Rosa glauca*, and perilla. More narrow steel trellises, twelve feet in height, appear here down the back of the border, twined with clematis. "I want to get the scale up," Lee says, explaining why she uses so many tall structures as well as big plants. "I never have many ditsy plants, they don't work for me. I look *down* into my garden." For the same reason, she favors colors like yellow that "will jump out at me as much as possible," and "poison green," Lee's name for that most useful color in the garden, chartreuse.

"I dug this garden when I was young and feisty," Lee recalls. "It was only half as deep at first. Then I added half as much again with a stone path going down the middle." About five years ago, with the help of Jim Hickey who mows the grass, Lee terraced the slope below the flower garden, "because I was so tired of everything just rolling down the hill." A panel of flat lawn now runs between the flower border and a

Lines of bluestone, set on edge and sunk to hold grass treads in the sloping lawn, curve down past retaining walls to the ten-foot-wide flower border below the house. Lee mixed bold-foliaged perennials, annuals, and shrubs here, using hues of dark red, clear yellow, cream, lavender, and chartreuse with the dusky plum foliage of purple smokebush and *Rosa glauca*.

narrow pool or rill she made, which is supported by another stone retaining wall. "It's just an old plastic baggie," she says of the stone-edged rill, a place for fish and water. Lee planted weeping mulberries at each end of the pool and more recently added two fastigiate hornbeams for height. "In doing all this, I was thinking of framing out the house. It's so tall, it needed to be softened," Lee remarks. "It's made all the difference. As you come up the hill, the trees focus your eye on the house."

Lee feels strongly that the relationship of the garden to the house is vital. "When I look at gardens in books and magazines," she says, "I find I want to know where I am. We've all seen delphiniums, but

we don't know how that person is seeing them." On the other hand, it takes time to work out a garden's design. "I've never understood people who can buy a house and immediately put in a garden," Lee says, having more patience than most of us. "I think you have to live there for a while."

When the summer porch was completed, Lee noticed right away that the front of the house looked lopsided. But it was a few years before she convinced Fritz of the need for a conservatory wing on the other end of the house to balance the porch. "I'd always thought I wanted a conservatory," she says quietly. She started leafing through books and conferring with her good friend, antique dealer Michael Trapp, who was building a similar room for himself. He found for Lee the tall narrow glass doors that Stan has combined to make the long windows of the room. The result is a high-ceilinged, sunlit, spacious entrance to the house in summer that doubles as a winter garden. With a fireplace at one end, it serves, too, as the winter dining room when it is crammed with plants. "You can barely get in there in the wintertime," Lee says, because of all the potted plants and the cuttings she does for the garden. Another small terrace has been laid outside the conservatory where Lee stages vignettes of potted plants. "These additions are what

make the house special," she stresses, "opening it to the outdoors."

"You know what the next project is?" Lee asks me, smiling. "A greenhouse. Off the garage. It doesn't have to be large. I want to do more things from seed." Stan's wife, Agnes, helps Lee with the gardening these days indoors and out. "She has a good eye," Lee says. "It's so much fun to work with someone who's young. It's a collaboration."

"Gardening is what I do in the country," Lee says simply. "I'm not a club person.

A conservatory was added onto the house on the opposite end from the summer porch. It serves as a winter dining room as well as a place to grow plants and cuttings indoors. It is also the sun-filled entrance to the Links' house.

Fritz will go play nine holes of golf, then he'll come home for lunch. I call that very civilized. Fritz is a city person. This isn't his heartbeat. It is mine."

The only drawback I can see to living in this picturesque part of Connecticut is that it is very buggy here—you cannot comfortably sit outdoors much of the spring and summer. "You should see me when I garden," Lee remarks with a laugh. "I wear long pants, clogs, turtlenecks, a bandana, a hat and goggles." But sitting on the summer porch, protected from the bites of gnats, black flies, and mosquitoes, you feel magically connected to the outdoors. The gardens, fields, and rolling hills stretch in front of you, surround you with their lush color and drama. "I love sitting here," Lee says. "It's very like theater, with the screen serving as a scrim." ■

A stone-paved entrance terrace was made in the angle of the new conservatory wing and the main part of the house, and is framed by boxwood hedging, grasses, and ferns. A decorative pot in the middle of the terrace is on axis with the entrance path and the French doors. On an old table beneath a bay window, Lee arranges vignettes of potted plants.

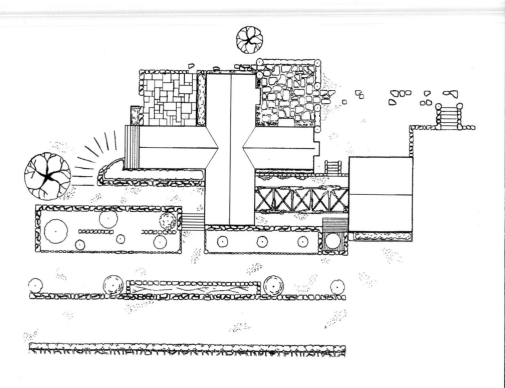

IT IS CONSIDERED a coup in Phoenix, Arizona, when you are building a house, to find a plot of land that borders up to or, even better, encompasses a desert wash. This arroyo, or dry creek, collects many more inches of rain water than the surrounding land, and consequently the native plants of the desert grow lustily here, creating a patch of wilderness and a habitat for wildlife. John and Ellen Giddens Stiteler found just such a desirable piece of land on which to build their house. "We were looking for a piece of land that was pristine in its desert integrity, but was not too far from John's office in downtown Phoenix, and we were lucky to find this, virtually still in town," Ellen said. It is a long rectangular lot, almost two acres in size, bounded on three sides by streets, with a spectacular view north and south of the Sonoran mountains. The desert wash, which contains several mature native trees, stretches across half the property. An easement meant that they couldn't build on that part of the land, but the Stitelers would not have dreamed of destroying its beauty. The rest of the property had been "bladed," Ellen says, scraped clean of all plant life. It was a vacant arid spot filled with debris. Here they would site their house.

The Stitelers built a starkly handsome contemporary dwelling with huge expanses

Desert Courtyards

Steve Martino Captures the Native Landscape

of glass in order to look out onto the arroyo and the mountains. Then they called on landscape architect Steve Martino to replant the barren areas around their house, and develop outdoor living spaces that would celebrate their piece of native landscape.

It is the sort of natural environment Steve loves, the landscape he has been championing and reinventing for the last twenty years. By bringing the desert into gardens

A graceful palo verde and tall, jagged ocotillo play against the Barragan-inspired walls of the Stitelers' house in Phoenix, Arizona. Landscape architect Steve Martino brings the plants of the surrounding Sonoran desert into the courtyards he designs.

and yards, onto terraces and patios, Steve has proven to homeowners how utterly suitable, how visually dramatic and appealing, the plants of their surrounding habitat are in such settings. The silhouettes of ocotillo, agave, prickly pear, and mesquite are striking seen against the masonry façades and courtyards of Arizona's houses. The graceful green-trunked desert tree, palo verde, and the gray-leaved shrubby brittlebush soften the hard architectural edges and bloom golden yellow in the spring. Scarlet salvias, agastaches, and penstemons attract a myriad of hummingbirds. Most important, all of these plants survive, indeed flourish, on the notoriously paltry annual seven inches of rain in Phoenix.

The Stitelers needed no convincing of the merits of desert planting. Steve's mission was to connect their house to the outside by creating courtyards for entertaining, then to dress those inner garden spaces with desert

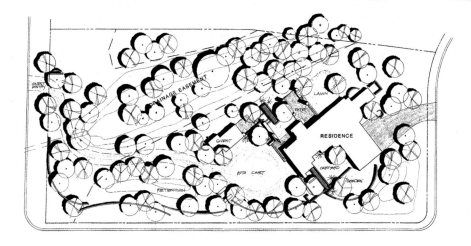

plants that would be a visual link with the nature beyond. First, Steve sited the driveway to run along the desert wash, wending past its mesquite, ironwood, goldeneye, and brittlebush. He repeated these gray-green plantings along the other side of the crushed stone drive, and continued planting them in drifts through the rest of the property that borders the streets and surrounds the house. He built long curving segments of masonry wall, three feet high, to overlap and seemingly interlock, forming a boundary between the property and the street without obscuring a view across the street of desert plantings and the mountains in the distance. The driveway leads to a starkly simple entry courtyard where two large spreading palo verdes, a few plump brittlebushes, and a tall jagged ocotillo, planted in the crushed stone, play against the bold architecture of the house.

At first glance the Stiteler's home seems much larger than it really is, appearing as an imposing two-story façade of smooth masonry painted the same warm taupe brown as the crushed stone in the driveway. In fact, it is simply a one-story, one-bedroom house, built, as Ellen says, "for the two of us." The spacious, high-ceilinged living room and dining area create a false impression of something more grand and complex from outside. To the left of the house and linked to it by a masonry wall painted a vivid orange, a

guest house provides quarters for friends and family. It sits at right angles with the main house, helping to frame the entry courtyard, and affording from its back windows and door a private view of the desert wash.

If you push open and pass through the tall pivoting iron-grid gate leading to the front door, you find yourself in the first of the two inner courtyards Steve created. This north-facing courtyard has no walls around it, opening instead freely onto the treasured arroyo. An outdoor patio for dining is on a direct axis with the glass doors leading out from the kitchen. Here, a round wooden table and six iron chairs, painted a copper brown, are shaded underneath an arbor made of perforated steel screening over steel beams held up by massive, angular masonry columns. The bold arbor frames the view beyond of desert plantings and the Sonoran mountains. The old specimens of mesquite, ironwood, and palo verde in the arroyo provide adequate privacy from the neighboring houses.

Steve planted another specimen mesquite tree, graceful in outline with striking rough, dark red bark, alongside the dining area to break the architectural starkness of the arbor. Just beyond, on axis with the large living room window, he built a narrow reflecting pool that juts out into the tree-filled wash and again leads your eye to the mountain setting. Twelve inches deep, it

is primarily decorative; but Steve points out that it is also for the Stiteler grandchildren to play in. One long side of the pool has a lip one-foot wide, suitable for sitting. The opposite side is slanted with no lip, causing the water to come up to the very edge and appear mirror-like. Steve quips about plagiarizing the Mexican architect, Luis Barragan, who is one of his mentors, and designed similar pools in the 1950s. In fact, much at the Stitelers is reminiscent of Barragan's work, from the smooth stark masonry façades, the brilliant stroke of orange wall,

A private courtyard inside the house entrance opens onto the desert landscape of the arroyo. Steve designed a reflecting pool here outside the living room windows that is on axis with a second pool and fountain in a courtyard on the opposite side of the room.

Right: An outdoor dining area under a perforated steel arbor is on direct axis with the glass doors leading from the kitchen. The severe lines of its architecture contrast with the wild scenery of the arroyo and Sonoran mountains. When Steve first started designing desert gardens twenty years ago, he used arroyos as his models. A specimen mesquite, above, similar to those occuring naturally in the desert wash, was planted between the arbor and pool.

and, indoors, the bold garden views framed by large windows of glass.

Steve sited another long spare pool in the courtyard on the south side of the house, placing it on axis with the north pool, so that you see it out the opposite glass wall in the living room. This courtyard is completely enclosed with walls, a private, intimate gravel terrace shaded by lacy palo verde trees, with water splashing softly from a fountain, and only a glimpse of Camelback Mountain above the walls. "The two courtyards are so different," Steve remarks, "the one like a fortress, the other all open." Rather than using a continuous wall to surround the secluded south courtyard, he enclosed it

with segments of walls that interweave—a typical trademark of Steve's. The blue-black fountain wall at the end of the pool hides a view of the street beyond, as well as a small adjacent back area devoted to vegetables and flowers. Here, out of sight—for they would surely be out of context—John and Ellen grow the tomatoes, lettuces, and roses they miss when not at their summer home in Connecticut.

All the colors in the courtyards are muted earth tones and silvers and greens, except for an occasional spattering of vivid yellow, red, or orange from a blooming salvia or Mexican honeysuckle. The same is true indoors where the colors seem to reflect the mountains in shadow. The furniture is in tones of taupe and beige, and the walls are painted the same warm brown as they are outside. But wonderful touches of color appear in the art and artifacts collected and displayed by the Stitelers. Ancient Native American figures, or kachinas, and bowls and rattles show strokes of turquoise and yellow. Warhol portraits of Western heroes and Native Americans lining the fireplace wall flash bold splashes of red and orange. The result is that the furnishings fade and what strikes your eye as you stand in the living room is the desert artwork inside and the dramatic landscape outside. It all seems of a piece. Steve speaks of the Stitelers' place

as an "expression of the relationship between southwestern culture and the desert."

Wherever you are in the house, you have a stunning view outdoors. Whether you are in the bathtub or at the kitchen counter or around the dining room table, your attention turns to the desert plantings, the pools, the craggy blue-red mountains. The house, with its outdoor living spaces, Steve says "embraces what's beyond."

"New design," he feels, "can be artful and at the same time nurturing to the envi-

The courtyard on the far side of the living room is completely enclosed by linked segments of walls, affording privacy from the street. The interweaving of short lengths of a wall (or a hedge), rather than the use of one solid barrier, often creates a more interesting effect. Left: A fountain adds a cooling sound, and a palo verde throws shadow patterns on the walls. Steve often points out the importance of silhouettes in a sunny garden.

The glass walls of the living room and dining room dramatically connect the interior to the desert courtyards and the mountains in the distance. Southwestern art and artifacts, strikingly displayed indoors, further link the house to its environs.

ronment." Furthermore, in Arizona it makes sense ecologically and economically to plant native plants. "A lot of the houses here just *consume* energy," Steve laments. Leaf blowers appall him. Fertilizers, he thinks, are better used on food crops. "The lawn is the most bizarre thing in the world," he says. "Billions of dollars go into growing lawn grass, then billions are spent chopping it down!" Steve likes to remind us that Phoenix gets just a few pathetic inches of rain a year and has endless stretches of searing heat. It is a strange environment for growing emerald lawns, impatiens, palms, and bougainvillea. He rails against landscape architects who "think nothing of the burden of maintenance. They burden their clients with tremendous overhead," planting non-natives that require extensive irrigation. "Desert plants just fit here," Steve says. Then, as a surprise bonus, native creatures come and activate the garden, creating a habitat.

Steve says when he sets out to design a garden he has three goals. First, to solve the site problems and satisfy the homeowners' needs. Second, to make a contribution to the street and to the environment. Third, to have fun, do something artistic. "Going the step beyond," Steve calls it. This he achieves in the imaginative configuration of his walls, pools, and gates. He likes to say that he does "non-landscape architecture." He puts in "the man-made elements, then lets nature fight it out."

Hardscaping—creating the permanent features of a garden—is almost always

Above: Colorful Native American rattles on a window ledge are silhouetted against the graceful mesquite, pool, and arbor.
Right: The mirror-like pool leads your eye from the house to the desert landscape. Twenty-four-feet long and twelve-inches deep, it also provides amusement for visiting grandchildren.

of prime importance. When you start designing your garden, figure your steps and paths, walls and water features first. Then soften the architecture of your garden with plantings that are suitable for your climate. Finally, when all is in place, let nature mess up your design a bit.

"I like to see my gardens go to wrack and ruin," Steve often says with a grin. When the prickly pears get big like giant Mickey Mouse ears, the ocotillos throw wriggly shadows, the brittlebushes sprawl, and the salvias and penstemons seed all over the stony ground, Steve feels his bold walls and pools, his broad steps, and crushed stone terraces, have nicely settled in. ■

JUST AS STEVE Martino likes to bring the desert right up to the doorstep of the house when he creates a garden in Arizona, so Sue Dixon wanted to be able to open her door to an expanse of the prairie she has always loved. "I don't have a garden," she told me firmly, at her home outside Chicago. I persuaded her that indeed she did, even if there were no borders or beds, no lawns, no topiary or hedges. Surely she lived in a garden, even though the prairie grasses and flowers she nurtured and allowed to spread all round her house were wild.

"I used to walk here," Sue explained to me, waving her hand out over the field of sawtooth sunflowers and prairie dock, cord grass, and big bluestem that is now her backyard—long before she and her husband, Wes, bought the land and built their house. Sue would pass the privately-owned five-acre piece of natural prairie on her way to the local nature preserve, The Lake Forest Open Lands—a two-hundred-acre sweep of virgin Illinois prairie surrounded by the original climax oak woodland. Wide paths are kept mowed through the shoulder-high grasses in the preserve, so residents can walk there with their dogs and in summer be nose-to-nose with the tall swaying wildflowers. It is a place Sue Dixon loves and where for years she would come to walk with her golden

Backyard Prairie

Sue Dixon's Wild Garden

retrievers. On her way home, she would linger on that adjacent five acres.

"I was standing out in the cattails," Sue remembers, one fateful day, "thinking how great it would be to have a home here. Wes thought I was crazy." The Dixons, after all, lived very comfortably in the family house they built in 1955—a half a block away. "We lived just down the street in a very

Sue Dixon wanted her new house in Lake Forest, Illinois, to open onto a patch of the prairie she has always loved. She and her husband willingly left behind a traditional garden of cultivated flowers and manicured edges at their former home, and set about restoring five acres of wet prairie to be their new backyard.

47

traditional house surrounded with gardens that were totally cultivated. We had no intention of ever moving; that is, until I had this idea." It would take a few years to carry it out.

When twenty-five acres of grasslands that belonged to a neighbor were being sold off to friends in small parcels, a young couple bought the five-acre lot that Sue had her eye on, and began to build a house on it. Illness caused them to stop, then the acreage was sold again. "It just sat there for a long time," Sue recalls. In the end, Sue was able to convince her husband of the excitement and pleasure of having a new home in a piece of prairie, and finally they bought the land eleven years later. With children long out of the nest, and the time now to enjoy a freer, less fettered lifestyle, Sue didn't want to be tied to a garden, at least not one with edges and the daily demands of upkeep. The

The Dixons' restored grasslands are adjacent to a preserve of virgin prairie. In the wettest corner of their own property, overrun with buckthorn, landscape designer Cliff Miller helped them create a pond. Using earth from the excavation, he designed a gently-rising knoll on the street side of the house and planted it with wildflowers and shrubs found in a native bur-oak savanna.

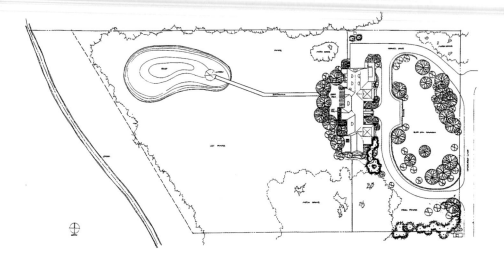

Dixons love to travel the world, and spend at least three months of the year at their ranch in Nevada where Sue breeds Arabian horses. While other couples at a similar stage in life might be considering slowing down, Sue and Wes Dixon are bursting with energy and a sense of adventure.

Having bought the land, the Dixons tore down the shell of the existing house and built a long, low-slung wooden home, facing west, that opens out onto the aspen-rimmed prairie. The house has the look of a handsome rustic lodge, glorified in size, darkly wooden, with bold fieldstone chimneys cutting its western façade and cedar decking that laps out into the landscape. A few tall aspens and smaller Freeman maples planted by the house help it to nestle into its wild setting. "When we built the house we didn't want it perched up over the site," Sue points out. "We lowered the house below ground on the east side so we would seem snuggled in here." You step down a good four feet when entering the Dixons' spacious, comfortable home from the driveway, only to find yourself drawn across the rooms to the great glass windows and sliding doors that look out onto the panorama of wildflowers and grasses. It is impossible to resist opening the doors and walking out onto the deck where the wide view is framed by gray-stemmed dogwoods and fluttering aspens.

Sue and Wes called on landscape architect P. Clifford Miller to restore their patch of prairie and design decking that would connect the house to the land. Cliff specializes in integrating homes into their sites in a naturalistic style. "But not too many clients let you do something this extreme," he admits. "The Dixons had an understanding of what the prairie is about," Cliff continues; they recognized and thrilled to its biodiversity, how even a small stretch of grasslands supports a wealth of species from wildflowers and the butterflies they attract, to an astonishing assortment of birdlife, insects, and animals. Cliff's goal was to strengthen the ecosystem by renovating the existing prairie, removing invasive foreigners like lythrum, and pushing back the brush—woody plants such as buckthorn and bur oak.

Through the wettest part of the property, at the aspen and bur oak treeline, a branch of the meandering Chicago river once ran—before farmers at the turn of the century dug a ditch to drain the land. Here, the Dixons and Cliff built a pond. "The site of the pond was already degraded," Cliff says in defense of this change; it was only buckthorn there. "We dug the pond from within so we had an immediate edge of plants," Cliff continues, reminding me why so many man-made ponds, scraped of plant life, look unnatural and out of place. With

the displaced soil from the pond site, Cliff created a knoll on the eastern side of the house, across the drive from the entrance, successfully screening the house from the street. Here he planted a bur oak savanna, a drier prairie environment where black-eyed Susans, goldenrod, and asters flourish.

"I immersed myself in this land until I understood it," Cliff told me, referring to his study of the great midwestern grasslands. With an understanding of this natural community, Cliff feels he has an advantage over the typical architect. "It allows me to step

The rustic low-slung house was deliberately sited below ground level so it would seem to nestle into the land. Tall native aspens planted near the house also give it a settled air. Choosing a species of tree indigenous to the landscape helps connect the house to its surroundings.

into those sites very softly." The noted landscape architect and teacher, Darrel Morrison, who creates startlingly contemporary designs using only the native plants of the region where he is working, was an inspiration for Cliff. I thought of Darrel as Cliff was talking, remembering a story he once told of camping out on a site in Texas for several days to get the sense of the place before he started his design.

Having established the pond and restored the prairie, Cliff turned his attention to the other crucial requisite: connecting the house with its setting. The original design of a deck, on the western front of the house facing the prairie, called for a mere catwalk. It was expanded to be a broad platform, thirty feet by sixty feet, that extends out from the main rooms of the house, a place where family and guests can relax, eat, have drinks, and savor the view. "We live out here," Sue admits. From this spacious cedar deck, steps lead down to a smaller platform with built-in wooden benches, and from there onto a narrow boardwalk, 150-feet long, that runs right out into the high grass and wildflowers, ending at the quiet lily-studded pond. "We walked the deck out into the prairie," Cliff says. Curved benches at the end of the walkway tempt you to linger by the water, hidden there by the tall grasses, entranced by the wildness and serenity.

Not only do the Dixons have an ever-changing panorama of flowers to enjoy from their wild garden, upkeep is at a minimum. No staking, no deadheading, no edging. And no watering is required, except for newly-planted trees up by the house. "Five or six years ago," Wes told me, "we had a terrible drought. All the neighbors' lawns were brown. Our prairie was green." The Dixons do keep a keen eye out for the dreaded purple loosestrife, pulling it out before it can spread. And they are careful to keep woody plants from encroaching in the grasslands.

A broad cedar deck, thirty feet-by-sixty feet, extends out from the main rooms of the house and is a favorite vantage point for viewing the daily-changing panorama of prairie life. The deck is an ideal transition between the wooden prairie-style house and its wild grassland garden.

Sue's prairie is burned every two years. This prevents shrubs and trees from invading. It also keeps some of the more aggressive wildflowers like goldenrod and sunflowers from dominating. The Native Americans once burned for better grasses, for they knew that in the process the earth was cleaned of dead grasses, and the soil enriched. The burning also encourages the production of flower heads and seeds. In nature, of course, prairies catch on fire from lightning storms. "We burn in late March or early April," Sue told me, "before the nesting season." Very carefully, Cliff added, with hoses at the ready. "It's a renewal," he says, giving the prairie "a cleaner look." Cliff went on to say that they guide the natural growth, but "we don't control it. The prairie is an incredibly dynamic ecosystem," all on its own.

Walt Whitman called the prairie "North America's characteristic landscape," because of its uniqueness. Nothing quite like it occurs in other parts of the world. According to architectural critic Paul Goldberger, Frank Lloyd Wright loved to say that "the only true American places were out on the prairie or in the desert." Here, in these two landscapes, he chose to build his homes, Taliesin and Taliesin West, in such a way that they embraced the land. Wright believed fervently in the importance of connecting the house with its land. His houses were

powerfully horizontal, Goldberger points out, because "to Wright, verticality meant going away from the land, and horizontality meant connecting to it." The houses, built in what he called his Prairie Style, "are set beneath low hipped roofs, with wide overhangs, and almost all of them have multiple windows and doors opening out to the land." The Dixons' house, with its long low profile and generous windows and doors, its deck and boardwalk, follows these principles.

For the Dixons, living surrounded by a fragment of this vanishing wilderness is a

Steps lead down from the spacious deck outside the house to a smaller platform with built-in benches, and from there to a narrow boardwalk, 150-feet long, which lures you out among the tall grasses, sawtooth sunflowers, Turks cap lilies, liatris and Joe-Pye weed. The boardwalk ends at the pond, where more benches on a small platform tempt you to linger.

daily thrill. "Brilliant skies this morning, and the prairie was a shining blanket of blue, white and yellow flowers," Sue writes in early July. In June, it's solid blue with spider-wort (*Tradescantia ohiensis*). Earlier in spring, marsh phlox bloom with blue flag iris. Dusty-pink Joe-Pye weed and blue lobelia (*L. siphilitica*), red-orange turkscap lilies and purple rattlesnake master (liatris) color the Dixon's prairie in late summer. And through summer and fall, the native sunflowers add blazes of yellow. The Dixons have named their place Prairie Dock ("our dock in the prairie," Sue says, enjoying the play on words) after the flower of that name—a tall daisy-like sunflower (*Silphium terebinthinaceum*), with huge, basal leaves shaped like elephant ears, that blooms in their high grass from July through September. With the future in mind, they have put their beloved five acres in a conservation easement so it can never be built on.

"We like to have parties out here on the deck," Sue remarks. "We'll have dinner and a band," for dancing, with fireflies overhead and the rustle of aspens. "At one party," Wes recounts, "one of our guests said: 'When are you going to get rid of these weeds?'" Wes laughs at the memory of it, knowing you can't explain to everyone the beauty of living in a patch of wildness.

Standing on their deck, confident in the wisdom of what they've done, Sue announces, deadpan, her eyes sparkling: "In our dotage, we can take our wheelchairs and come out here into the prairie." ▪

The lily-studded pond is a delightful destination on walks from the house through the prairie grasses and flowers. Cliff Miller and the Dixons were careful to dig the pond from the center out, in order not to disturb its natural edging of plants. Consequently, it looks completely natural. Only the weeping willows are not indigenous to the scene, although they flourish in this watery site.

WHEN SHE MOVED to her new home in Bedford, New York, four years ago, Laura Fisher did not intend to have a flower garden. She had left a large, lavish garden behind, one that required a staff to maintain. Now, she was determined to simplify—she would plant a few choice trees near the house, and grow evergreens in patterns, which had to be clipped only once or twice a year. At her former home, gardening had been her creative outlet. Now she wanted the time to devote to her new passion—designing fabrics with floral motifs using an ancient Japanese dyeing technique called *katazome*.

An old barn on her present property, which was a short walk from the house, seemed an ideal place to set up a studio. Laura had French doors installed where there had been big barn doors on either end, to let the light in and open the room up to the outside. Inside, the large, two-story space now holds her work table, where she creates her printed velvets. Elaborate fringes and buttons are piled in baskets and the velvets themselves, in gold, soft red, sage green, silvery blue, lie crumpled on the table or draped from a second story balcony.

As she began working in her new room, Laura realized that she needed flowers close by to serve as inspiration for her

Studio Garden

Laura Fisher's Floral Patterns

textile designs. Despite her resolution, she decided to have a garden just outside her studio French doors—a small, exotic, flowery world. The ground in the old stable yard was hard pan, and consequently difficult to dig by hand. "A man with a back hoe was doing some drainage work for me," she recalls. "I asked him if he could dig me some beds in the gravel outside the studio. So he handed me a can of spray paint, and I drew

Laura Fisher planted an exotic mixture of flowers and vines on either side of the path to her studio. Not only does she enjoy their colors and patterns as she walks by or glances through her studio windows, but they serve as inspiration for her floral textile designs.

Right: Long-handled bottlebrush gourds edge the gravel path together with dark perilla and silver helichrysum. The bold leaves of the gourds help give structure to this luxuriously busy garden. White buddleias and sunflowers bloom with gladiolas and cannas in September. Above: A Victorian stone table and seat, as well as pots of flowers and sprawling annuals, blur the edges of the two rectangular beds.

two big rectangular beds." The beds, dug and enriched, are now filled with a wonderfully wild, eclectic mixture of plants. Regal white and yellow gladiolas, dark red dahlias and scarlet cannas, as well as delicate lilies, like her favorite orange *Lilium henryi*, rise through a thicket of annuals and biennials that Laura lets seed about lavishly in the two beds—poppies, sweet rocket, feverfew, perilla, angelica, *Verbena bonariensis*, and *Coreopsis tinctorum*. A tropical-looking twelve-foot-high aralia (*A. cordata*) with greenish-white tufts of flowers followed by purple berries in fall, and equally tall white impatiens, *I. glandiflora*, add, along with sunflowers, astonishing height in

58

summer considering the fact that they are tender and die back to the ground each winter. White-flowering buddleias also add stature in late summer, mingling with willowy pink and purple New England asters.

"I've always gardened mixing hardy plants with half-hardy perennials and annuals," Laura says. "I like the length of time annuals flower." She also likes the fact that they seed themselves. "I love the surprises," she says. Their vibrant colors are another advantage. "When I first started gardening," Laura recalls, "I stuck to pastels. Now I like bold colors. I like to see what I can get away with." One thing that happens as we mature as gardeners, is that our taste for color gets more audacious. We tire of the easy soft hues, and crave something more daring, something immodest, to give the garden a punch.

Laura's forte outdoors, first learned from her friend, designer Hitch Lyman, is in creating a garden that is shamelessly luxurious in color, and startling, adventuresome, in its juxtaposition of plants. "I always say my garden is like my hair," she says with a smile. In both cases, the end result is seemingly out-of-control, romantically disarranged. "You need a shoehorn to get anything more in the

Left: Laura's work table stands in the center of the old two-story barn that she converted into a studio. She replaced the huge sliding barn doors with French doors, opening her workroom to the garden outside. In summer, she takes detailed photographs of the flowers and vines that particularly please her eye. These images she uses in winter when she composes her fabric designs. She also loves the surprises in her garden, such as the vines that climb unexpectedly into a neighboring plant, above.

garden, because I can't stand it to look bare or too neat," Laura adds. She encourages an interweaving, a veritable tangle, of plants. Like many artistic gardeners who enjoy letting nature have a hand in how the garden arranges itself, however, Laura edits the results. "I pull out tons of the impatiens and

A freshly-gathered bouquet of asters shares the worktable with the tools of Laura's textile art. Patterns of vines and flowers from her garden are transferred to lengths of velvet by an ancient Japanese process of stenciling and dyeing called *katazome*.

feverfew as the garden fills in." She waits for a misty day to pull out an excess of favorite plants like the native blue lobelia (*L. siphilitica*), and transfers this to pots, together with delphiniums, fragrant white tuberose, and sky-blue *Salvia uliginosa*.

Pots of these and other assorted flowers and vines are staged along the gravel path to the studio. "I don't want to see a lot of gravel," Laura says, "and I don't want regular edges, so I use pots of flowers to give the front of the borders an irregular line." She also encourages annuals to sprawl. Silvery helichrysum, maroon perilla, flame-colored nasturtiums, and bold-leafed gourds romp in waves on either side of the path. "My favorite things for the border edges are these long-handled birdhouse gourds because of their foliage," Laura states. "I need some big leaves because the garden is so busy," and this summertime vine gives the needed structure to frame the garden. "The vines grow so quickly that I've often thought if I laid down on the path and slept there for the night, they'd grow right over me!" Laura loves the fact that the garden is small enough for her to weed herself. "I never feel overwhelmed by it."

One September afternoon when I was visiting, Laura pointed out a tiny scarlet cypress vine (*Ipomoea quamoclit*) that had unexpectedly wound around the stalk of a pale yellow gladiola in a terracotta pot. "I like when vines climb over other things," she remarked. As we stood admiring the cypress climber, she pointed out that its sharply-lobed palmate leaves almost looked like birds in their shape and movement. "Every time I walk down to the studio in the morning, it thrills me," she says of her intimate and enveloping pathway garden. "I'm completely lifted in spirit. I can linger there quietly when I want to feel calm and centered."

When Laura sees something in the garden that she particularly likes, she photographs close-ups of it. In winter, she'll sit down in her studio with the accumulated photographs of flowers, vines, and leaves, and compose designs from them for her fabrics. Then she hand cuts stencils based on her designs. A paste is squeezed through the stencil onto the fabric, blocking out "the negative space," leaving the flower image exposed to color by hand. This sixteenth-century Japanese process of dyeing fabrics gives Laura far more flexibility with color combinations than she would have using a silk screen where the repeated image is static. Hand painting the floral designs with dyes is "more like oil painting," she says. The resulting fabrics are sumptuous and personal. Recognizable images of vines and flowers—clematis, lupines, delphiniums—are picked out in silver and blue, in one

instance, against a background of shimmering sea-blue velvet. Or gold leaves and vines might be painted on a velvet of soft Venetian red. Laura fashions her finished fabrics into shawls and scarves, adding antique tassels and beads.

"Both my art and my garden are a process," she says. "The difference is the garden is so ethereal." Its imprint is there, nonetheless, in her beautiful fabrics. ■

Laura's shawls and scarves capture her ethereal artistry with the plantings outside her studio doors.

A WEEKEND HOME in Tuxedo Park, to me, conjures up visions of a vast Edwardian shingled house, perched on a hillside, with a dozen bedrooms and wraparound porches that afford views of pine and oak forest, a shimmering lake, and, possibly, in the misted distance as if from another world, the Manhattan skyline. Such a house is the norm in this gated enclave where, since before the turn of the century, the wealthy have escaped for summer. So, arriving for the first time at Joe and Anne McCann's hideaway here, I was astonished to find a tiny toy of a house, not shingle but stucco, painted a playful yellow, tucked away at the foot of a hill of ledge rock, with no more expansive view than one of a neighbor's meadow where deer graze in the early morning sun. Their property is a mere 100 feet by 150 feet, a postage stamp by Tuxedo Park standards.

The McCanns' diminutive house is a former garage, all that remains of a cluster of outbuildings that belonged to one of those great turn-of-the-century piles; the wooden structures were destroyed by a fire in the 1930s. When Joe and Anne discovered the property fifteen years ago, only this stucco garage remained standing, its tall doors sealed closed; fifty feet beyond it yawned the two-story-deep stone retaining walls and foundation of the servants' house, stable,

Garden in a Ruin

Anne and Joe McCann's Weekend Retreat

and smokehouse, filled with the collapsed debris of the fire.

Realizing that the slate-roofed garage was a size perfectly suited to their needs, as weekenders without children, the McCanns purchased the place. "We were looking for the opposite of a trophy house," Joe explains. "We lived in the city after all. We didn't want something overwhelming. Rather, we wanted something simple." Anne adds: "And

Anne and Joe McCann spend their weekends gardening, cooking, and reading at their home in a wooded setting an hour's drive from New York City. Their tiny stucco house is a former garage—all that remains of a cluster of outbuildings belonging to a turn-of-the-century estate that burned in a fire in the 1930s.

we wanted it to be fun." Not only charmed by the outline and size of the garage, they were intrigued by the adjacent stone ruins, appreciating its romantic aura and its potential eventually to become the bones of a garden.

Joe and Anne called on an architect friend, Michael Manfredi, to redo the inside completely and to create a connection between the house and future garden in the ruins. Former tenants had built a floor above the old concrete grease pit of the garage to make a living room. This was replaced by a new polished cherry-wood floor, raised eighteen inches above ground level to afford better views out the large turn-of-the-century windows set high along the side walls. Today, as you sit at the long dining table in the middle of the living room, you see across to fields in one direction, ledge rock and oak trees in the other, and down, through the old garage entrance, to the garden.

Two gracefully curved wooden steps lead down from the living area to bluestone paving that flows from inside out through the four original oversized doors. The doors are ten feet high, the lower half of wood, with glass panes at the top. Custom-made screens allow the doors to be flung open on warm summer days. Outside, the bluestone extends down the whole front of the house, joining wooden decking that leads to a gazebo and the stone walls of the ruins.

"It's a totally inside-outside situation," Joe announces grinning, as, with book in hand, he settles down in a lawn chair on the terrace outside the great doors. "Because there's not a lot of room inside."

One of the first things the McCanns did to extend the living space outdoors was build a gazebo on an elevated deck to one side of the house, above the old smokehouse. Manfredi and his partner, Michael De Candia, designed the gazebo to suggest the house in miniature. Four yellow stucco pillars support

The McCanns had a raised cherry-wood floor built above the former concrete grease pit in their new living room in order to enjoy the views from the large windows set high along the side walls. Custom-made screens make it possible to fling open the handsome old garage doors on warm days. Original heating pipes still run along the ceiling.

turquoise wooden shutters that Jennifer found and had cut to fit. From the entrance steps, a limestone path extends to the front gate, and is the center axis of the flower garden Jennifer created. "I did this garden five years ago for a wedding," she says. At that time, a couple was doing the tile work in the kitchen. "We became friends," she explains. "They were from England and wanted to get married here." Jennifer drew several designs on paper for the front garden, and chose the simplest one, a cross of paths with panels of grass surrounded by beds of flowers. Down the main path, she planted upright conifers native to Texas, 'Will Flemming' yaupons (*Ilex vomitoria*). "I thought of Monet's gardens," she says, "but instead of arches, yaupons." Jennifer and her husband, Fred, laid the paths with native stone. "There were tons of old stone in the woods that the previous owner had bought off an old homestead," Jennifer recalls. "We picked out pieces to make the paths. We did it with day laborers, a Mexican farmer and his sons, all working together."

A side path leads around to a new limestone terrace extending out from the back of the house. White Christmas tree lights are strung across the terrace for a festive evening air. "In the winter," Jennifer recounts, "I have fires out here and play Mexican music when we have a party." Two huge camellias in clay pots stand on the

terrace on either side of broad limestone steps Jennifer and Fred built that descend between rows of crab apples to the creek. From this vantage point the house looks like one you might see in a French village, a three-story pale stone façade with flowers spilling out of window boxes. An oval sculpture of three women, done locally, is placed here, along with a piece of driftwood from the Gaudelupe River, and a Corinthian plinth from a building in Chicago.

Left: The garden, with its lavish display of anemones and ranunculus in paintbox colors, spills right out of the front gate and on to the street. **Above:** The center axis of the garden, seen through the Myers' gracious front door, extends to the iron gate by the street. Central panels of grass separate the path from the borders of rioting flowers.

97

Artemisia 'Powis Castle', below, and ranunculus, above, are planted in sweeps. It is the lavishness of Jennifer's plantings that makes her garden so effective. Right: The bold foliage of cardoons, palms, and agaves contrasts nicely with the more ephemeral flowers.

Jennifer's schooling was primarily in art, but then she went to nursing school, "so I could earn a living," she states. Most days Jennifer works at the hospital tending heart patients. But on Fridays she gets into her lavender truck and goes to drawing class for several hours. Art is her passion.

Although she is shy about showing her drawings, her biggest canvases—her home and garden—are there for all to see, and she is delighted to share them with friends and acquaintances. The garden is enjoyed even by strangers passing by in cars or on foot. "This house is on the hike and bike trail. There's a detour from the creek that goes by my front gate. I've met some neat people on the trail just stopping while I'm out here gardening," Jennifer says.

What they see outside the gate is a large spiky agave in a pot, lantanas and salvias, and a dazzling display of her beloved anemones and ranunculus. "They don't come back, they're throw-away money," Jennifer says of these fabulous tender bulbs. Thinking of her extravagance, she adds: "The other nurses spend money on pocketbooks. I buy fifteen-hundred bulbs to plant instead."

Indeed it is the lavishness of her planting and the boldness of her sweeps of color that make Jennifer's garden so memorable. And then there is the added delight of finding the same spirit indoors. A bold vision, bravura, a certain artful abandon, and a sense of fun, are the requisites to achieve this merry visual impact, the lines between home and garden blurring in a shared explosion of color. ∎

SITUATED A FEW blocks across Austin from Jennifer Myers's place, Gordon White's house and garden are also of a piece, as successfully married in look and atmosphere as hers, and yet completely different. Whereas Jennifer's is merrily boisterous, busy and colorful, Gordon's is spare and serene, and dependent more on line and pattern than any display of color.

On my first visit to Gordon's home in old West Austin, I was captivated by its peaceful air and simple beauty even before I had reached the entrance door of the stucco house. Enclosed on all sides by fencing and stone walls, the one-quarter-acre property feels secluded as soon as you enter it from the street. While the other houses in this quiet urban neighborhood are fronted by the typical small rectangle of lawn and broad swath of paved driveway, at Gordon's, the lawn and the traditional driveway have been dispensed with. Instead, a Zen-like garden, patterned with a wave of flat limestone and swirls of raked gravel intermingled with choice plants, leads to the front door. Walking in from the street, you can stop to crouch by an exquisitely blooming South African bulb, or admire a gathering of decorative grasses, arranged with the delicate restraint of a Japanese watercolor.

This front driveway entrance was Gordon's first garden project when he moved

Garden of Serenity

Gordon White's Zen-inspired Refuge

to his new home in 1991. He persuaded a local artist and stone artisan, who had built the original stone steps and walls, to return and help him lay stone in the entrance area. Working over a period of two months, the two men pieced the great limestone slabs together, so they would seem to flow from the street to the garage at the side of the house. Around the limestone, they spread granite gravel one-quarter-inch deep (it lasts

Instead of the typical panel of lawn and asphalt driveway, the approach to Gordon White's house in West Austin, Texas, is a mosaic of limestone slabs and raked gravel, interspersed with choice bulbs, wildflowers, and perennials.

Above left: A ribbed vase and prostate pyracantha decorate the entrance steps to Gordon's house. The iron gate opens into a tiny courtyard and the front door. Above right: A venerable cedar elm (*Ulmus crassifolia*) by the entrance is underplanted with liriopes and holly ferns (*Cyrtomium falcatum*). Far right: The main axis of the garden runs from the front door through the house to the back deck and terrace. Evergreen *Clematis armandii* frames the doorway to the back garden.

somewhat longer than decomposed granite, Gordon says) and here Gordon planted a few special bulbs and perennials. A vertical rock and a ribbed vase stand in the gravel at one side of the broad limestone steps to the entrance gates, softened by the graceful stems of a prostrate pyracantha. "The house dictated the Eastern feeling of the garden," Gordon says.

The aura of Eastern serenity continues as you push open the green-painted iron gates, slip your shoes off in the tiny inner courtyard, and silently enter Gordon's spare,

sunlit rooms. The colors here are soft monotones, earth colors, but for the spines of books piled in inviting stacks, and the starkly poetic black and white photographs of female nudes, flowers, and trees, arranged in simple rows on the white walls or propped up on the floor.

As you walk through the house you are constantly aware of the garden outside. The front and back doors line up so that, upon entering, you immediately get glimpses down the hall out to the main axis of the garden. One eighteen-foot length of wall in the large living-dining room is glass sliding

doors that frame a small enclosed side garden. A series of light transoms over the doors, and two skylights cut in the hallway ceiling, allow even more light to flood the room and give glimpses of the old elms that stretch their great limbs across the property.

The house is furnished sparsely but thoughtfully. In the main room, a long antique sideboard stands against one wall; on it, Gordon has arranged still lifes of Japanese pottery, dried leaves, fresh flowers, and photographs. For the other end of the

Left: The twenty-by-thirty-foot living-dining room is as simply furnished and serene as the garden. The glass sliding doors and transoms along the east wall look out onto a small enclosed courtyard, above, planted with a native persimmon (*Diospyros*), Texas sage (*Leucophyllum*), and a dwarf blue agave.

room, he had a local artisan, Daniel Kagay, design an equally long dining table and eight chairs, providing a place for entertaining as well as desk work. No other furnishings clutter the light-filled space. Bedrooms, too, are spartan. A small book-filled library, however, holds two plump chairs and a sofa for reading by the fire, and the kitchen, sleek and modern, is equipped with every convenience for serious cooking. Gordon is a great reader and a dedicated cook as well as a passionate gardener.

Just outside the library, a deck for dining was built one foot up from ground level so as not to disturb the roots of the existing post oaks and cedar elms that handsomely arch over the house and the garden.

He is also one of Austin's most eminent neurosurgeons, and when he moved to Austin in 1991, after an internship and residency in New York, he sought a home that would be a refuge. This small, very private, contemporary house, enclosed by walls but open to its garden, seemed ideal to him. It had been built in 1980 by Sidney and Dean Kilgore, Texans with an interest in architecture and a love of gardens. "I was brought up with a Japanese aesthetic," Sidney explains, and this very much influenced their design. Collaborating with an architect, they sought to create a one-story dwelling in this urban spot, where a strong relationship existed between each room and an outdoor space, with natural light pouring indoors from all sides. "We called it the house of repose," Sidney says.

The house was constructed carefully within the established trees, splendid cedar elms and post oaks that fortunately existed on the narrow lot. When the foundation was being dug, Sidney would come over and drape damp blankets on any exposed roots of the great old trees. She loved them for their intrinsic beauty. But they also gave the house an instant legitimacy, an air of always having been there; and their cool shade is invaluable in the heat of a Texan summer.

Sidney asked the talented Austin landscape architect, James David, to help devise a garden plan once the house was finished.

Above: A gravel garden to one side of the deck is raked in swirled patterns around South African bulbs and perennials that have been planted and seed about. Right: Potted rose cuttings line the deck and are moved to capture the fleeting sunlight in this predominantly shady garden. The deck and gravel garden are enclosed by a high stucco wall topped by iron grilling that echoes the pattern of the transoms inside.

He developed the main axis of the garden, continuing the interior perspective that ran from front door to back. Out the back of the house, James suggested constructing a wooden deck rather than a terrace, in order not to disturb the tree roots of the over-hanging post oak. A spacious deck was raised one foot up from ground level just outside the library. Here Gordon now has a circular stone table and cypress chairs also crafted by Kagay for outdoor dining. Three easy steps down and you are in the garden, a walled

courtyard where the ground is graveled with stone richly warm in color—like pale cocoa—and flowers crop up seemingly at will. The plants here, whether deliberately planted, like the many spring and summer flowering bulbs from South Africa, or seeded unexpectedly like alyssum, violas, columbines, Peruvian lilies (*Alstroemeria*), and anthericum, dictate the pattern of the gravel.

A high stucco wall, topped with a galvanized steel grill that repeats the pattern of the transom windows indoors, encloses this area of deck and gravel garden and divides it from the back garden. Through a gateway draped with evergreen *Clematis armandii*, are glimpses of a green and shaded garden beyond, ending with a folly-like toolshed painted most recently a lively pattern of yellow and lime green. The toolshed and a bench in front of it, placed at the very back of the property, end the main perspective which runs from the front door of the house.

James David planned the original geometric pattern of the back garden, designing the peaked-roof toolhouse and a narrow pool in front of it, on line with the back door and gateway. This small rectangular fish pond is edged with stone and alternating strips of gravel and dwarf mondo grass. "All the lines move to the bench and to the little toolshed, emphasizing that this is where the eye stops," James points out. Sinuously horizontal branches of a great cedar elm (*Ulmus crassifolia*) interrupt the severity of this geometric garden area and create welcome shade. To the side of the toolshed and pool, a patch of lawn is edged with ornamental grasses and shrubs in varying textures of green.

Each time, however, I visit Gordon's garden, the size of the lawn has shrunk. Gordon is determined to get rid of all the grass eventually, no doubt in reaction to the effects of the brutal drought and unrelenting

Right: Passing through the doorway in the wall, you step down into a green and shaded back garden, featuring a fish pool and folly-like toolhouse, below. Gordon's garden plays more with pattern and texture than bright color.

heat of the last two summers. He is experimenting instead with evergreen plants in gravel, such as the clipped dwarf mugho pines and black monkey grasses, which he has planted in diagonal patterns. His partner in these experiments is an avid young plantsman, Steve Bell, who comes to help in the garden every Saturday. "He is so knowledgeable about plants," Gordon says admiringly. "I try to spend Saturday working side by side with him."

This is Gordon's first opportunity to make a garden, and he is thrilling to it. He grew up in Germantown on the outskirts of Philadelphia, in what was basically a row house with a minimal garden. "But my grandmother was an avid gardener. She lived in West Philadelphia on Fifty-Third and Pine, and had a garden there. We also used to play in the Awbury Arboretum nearby. When I left home I got into containers, but it wasn't until I bought this house that I really got into gardening."

"Gordon's a real minimalist," his good friend James David observes, pleased to see that he has made the garden his own. On a recent visit, I watched Gordon slowly rake the gravel in circles and waves around the plants and stone balls in his entranceway. It was a soothing occupation, precise and poetic, and, like so much of gardening, completely absorbing, allowing peaceful contemplation.

What could be more satisfying for a man who devotes most of his time to the challenge of saving lives.

It is thanks first to the vision of the original owners and designer, and finally to the vision enhanced and perfected by Gordon White, that here is a perfect example of a house that is connected to its garden not only physically but in atmosphere. A mood, an aesthetic, flows from one to the other without interruption. ▪

Austin landscape architect James David planned the strong axis of this quiet garden, drawing your eye—with the geometric lines of the pool, panels of gravel, and dwarf mondo grass— from the doors of the house to the toolshed at the end of the perspective. Branches of a great cedar elm break the formality of the pool area.

"I LOVE COLOR!" Liz Cheval said when she met with Craig Bergmann and James Grigsby to plan the garden at her newly purchased property in Lake Forest, Illinois. She had already drenched the elegant rooms indoors with pure, deep hues—vibrant red, velvety rust, rich green, and gold. She wanted the same saturated color outside, contained within the venerable existing evergreen framework. Craig was delighted, for a change, to work with a strong palette—most of his clients ask him for muted hues.

Craig is a talented garden designer and plantsman, who, with his partner, James, runs a thriving landscape business in the Chicago area. They readily agreed to collaborate on the renovation of Liz's property, knowing it was one of Lake Forest's historic residences. Built in 1908 in the Edwardian style, the house had been overhauled in the 1920s by W.A.P. Pullman to have a more "colonial" look, so popular at the time. A tiny picturesque cottage, built behind the house by the original owner as a place where her brother could go smoke his cigars, was attached by Pullman to the main building with a wing, making the house considerably grander.

Mr. Pullman was an avid horticulturalist, well-known for his hybridizing of evergreens—the hardy 'Pullman' boxwood, among them—and for helping to start the

Formal Rooms of Color

Craig Bergmann's Tapestries of Flowers and Foliage

Chicago Botanical Garden. It was he who established the wonderful bones of Liz's garden. Old boxwood parterres and hedges grace the grounds around the house in pleasing patterns, and great old yew hedging forms a backdrop for what was probably once—and is again—a lavish flower garden.

When Liz bought the house, it had been empty for many years. But, having had

A luxurious and richly-colored mixed border, backed by clipped boxwood and yew, curves around a center panel of lawn, and sets the stage for a garden-oriented house in Lake Forest, Illinois. Garden designers Craig Bergmann (above right) and James Grigsby (above left) are shown in front of their landscape studio.

terracing it into many different levels, planting as he went. The two lowest levels, no more than one foot from the dining room windows, are supported by stone retaining walls, into which he has tucked ferns and creeping flowers. Until recently, Larry kept two lop-eared rabbits on the ground level just outside the windows, and five hens had a run on top of the wall. Their antics were enjoyed from the dining room table. But their daily care made traveling on vacations difficult, so now plants flourish in the bunny run, and, on top of the wall, rows of vegetables have replaced the chickens—Swiss chard, parsley, and a variety of tomato called 'San Francisco Fog'.

A blue and neon-yellow painted wooden fence guides you up the first set of steps leading to a level parallel with the roof. From here, Larry has devised several series of wooden steps and paths that curve up the hillside, past a large handsome Capetown silver tree with velvety leaves (*Leucadendron argenteum*) underplanted with variegated abutilons and geraniums. A bench allows you to pause beneath a fernleaf Catalina ironwood tree with shaggy bark. At another bend in the path, up twelve more steps, you come upon a small fish pond with a gunnera spreading its immense fanlike leaves over it. The pond is known as the raccoon bath and smorgasbord, according to Larry, who is content to share his garden with the local wildlife. A large area of the hillside at this point is ingeniously retained by oak whiskey barrels, sliced in half, and piled on top of

When Larry and his partner bought the house eight years ago, the garden was nothing but weeds and brambles. Gradually Larry terraced the steep slope, and planted it with drought-tolerant species like the Capetown silver tree (*Leucadendron argenteum*), left. A large gunnera leans over a fish pond, above, and whiskey barrels cut in half hold up a section of the hillside, below.

Above: Larry's latest project was to build a room on his roof that would provide a splendid view of the cityscape on one side and the garden on the other. A bridge crosses over to the new room from the garden. Far right: At the top of the garden a platform serves as an aerie looking down over the lush foliage and flowers of the garden, and out across rooftops to the city and bay in the distance.

each other in several rows. Each barrel is filled with earth and spills with varieties of herbs and flowers—red spires of pineapple sage, the white and yellow cups of romnyea, flaming nasturtiums, and velvet purple *Salvia leucantha*. More wooden steps and a railing, wound about with white-flowering jasmine, lead steeply up the whiskey barrel slope to the final level, where they installed a hot tub and a platform from which to enjoy their most spectacular view. A tall wooden fence, along with several pine trees and a grove of bamboo, divides their property from their neighbor's, and serves as a screen behind the platform. From this highest part of the property, you look down across the wildly leafy garden, and over the rooftops, to the hazy blue city and glittering bay beyond.

The hot tub is a destination, Larry says, an excuse to walk up through the garden. I assumed he and Barry must spend hours up there, relaxing on the deck at the top of their aerie. But Larry said no, they only lingered for their dips in the tub. The climate is too chilly, too damp for lolling outside. San Francisco is full of micro-climates, and Noe Valley is on the edge of the sunbelt, which means it doesn't have as much fog as some neighborhoods. But the weather here is a far cry from the hot baking climate of Napa Valley, for instance, just over the bridge and on the other side of the mountains.

The design of the garden evolved more out of circumstance that any consideration for aesthetics, Larry explains. "I wanted to make a garden to amble through," with curving paths and different levels of planting, resulting in "the longest way possible to get to the hot tub." Larry calls it a plant person's garden, because of his tendency to collect plants, and his knowledge and love of unusual flora. Originally, gardening was Larry's vocation. In college, he turned from a major in psychology to horticulture, going on to study and work at The Chelsea Physic Garden in London as part of an independent masters program. "I was a horticultural vacuum cleaner," he says of those days. After a subsequent spell taking a certificate program of courses at Kew Gardens, he returned to the United States, and began to teach horticulture at San Francisco City College, and then at the University of California at Berkeley. But he found teaching too intense, and consequently went on to set up his own business—organizing national market research studies. "Gardening," he says, "is now a love, a hobby."

Larry grows many plants in the protea family—from the Cape of South Africa and southeastern Australia. These evergreen shrubs and trees, like Mediterranean plants, have similar cultural requirements to native California flora. "I was trying to make a primarily drought-tolerant garden," he says, "and lately we've had nothing but floods!" For the more normal dry spells in summer and fall, he has installed an irrigation system with a timer, and as a result, his garden is fairly low maintenance—requiring about two hours of work a week.

This summer, however, he worked hard on a new project. With a friend who is a structural engineer, Larry built a small room on his rooftop, from which you have a grand view of San Francisco on one side and a splendid prospect of his hillside garden on the other side. A wooden bridge spans the

Outside the new room on the roof, Larry grows lettuces, strawberries, and cuttings in recycled plastic pallets, which he punched with holes. A drip system of irrigation solves the watering problem.

gap between the garden path and the flat roof, which is now covered with wood chips. On the street side of the new roof room, just outside its window, Larry grows lettuces and strawberries in large black plastic pallets he salvaged at a recycling place. The pallets were made for fork lift trucks, and cost him two dollars each. He punched holes in them, filled them with soil mix, and sowed seed. Slugs, one of the city's scourges, will not be a problem up here on the rooftop, Larry suspects, surrounded as it is by open sky.

Larry likes having creative projects going whether they're woodworking or gardening, inside or outside. His newest scheme is to try creating a water course all the way down the garden from the hot tub to the dining room. With gardening, he says, "the nice thing is, there's no end to it. You can add and change and redo forever." His only regret is that his garden is hidden from the street. He wishes he had enough land in front to have "a great rock garden" out to the street, so he could talk to people as they walk by. "My garden is so tucked away—I'd like to share it with the street. So I plant as much as I can by our entrance."

Arching fronds of a large tree fern seem to burst from the yellow painted staircase that leads up one story from the sidewalk to the front door. A passion flower vine covers the wall at street level where

Larry has hung a mirrored window just for fun. Beneath it, a planter is filled with small-flowered fuchsias, a fragrant daphne, and seasonal bulbs. A Chinese fan palm serves as their diminutive street tree. The overall effect is welcoming and cheerful, and suggests that, indeed, a gardener lives here. Inside, a glance through the windows of the dining room to the garden wending up the hillside, tells the tale—that it is a whole, the gathering of flowers on the street side of the house hinting at the proliferation of plants behind its walls, which, even in a cool rain, is enjoyed from within. ■

A large tree fern explodes from the staircase of the house, painted playful colors of green, yellow, and blue. Passion flowers cover the wall at street level and surround a playfully hung mirrored window.

MARK INGMIRE lives in a one-story concrete-block tract house just like all the others on his street in South Miami. "But you'll recognize my place," he said, when I was coming to visit. "It's the only house you can't see." Mark's house is so densely camouflaged by palm trees—over fifty varieties he has grown from cuttings or seed—that, at first glance, you might think you are passing by a tiny tropical arboretum, partially hidden behind hedges and fencing. But a glimpse of an old pale-blue Volvo parked in the semblance of a driveway, mondo grass running down its center strip, and an arched wooden gateway in the fence, spiked with palm fronds, suggest something more.

Entering through the gate one April afternoon, with a picture still in my head of the neighborhood's parched brown lawns at this dry time of year, I found myself suddenly, and almost unbelievably, immersed in a shaded, romantic, lushly verdant tropical world. Water splashed down a series of rock ledges into a lily pond surrounded by explosions of elephant ears, bromeliads, staghorn ferns, birds-of-paradise, and an assortment of palms, some swaying high overhead, others standing squat and feathery. Black-foliaged begonias, dwarf mondo grass, and tradescantia covered the ground. A graveled path, edged with old ship's rope, curved through the trop-

Tropical Oasis

Mark Ingmire's Watery Jungle

ical foliage to the open house, through which you could see an expanse of water and a jungle of foliage and flowers on the other side. The effect was astounding, so completely had you entered another place, another time.

I had heard about Mark's house, how he had knocked all the walls out, so that it was literally open to the outside, except for a roof and a floor. The bedrooms and a bath do have walls, and the house can be closed up with sliding windows, if Mark leaves town;

Mark Ingmire transformed a concrete tract house on a suburban street in South Miami by knocking down the walls and opening it to a tiny jungle paradise he created with pools and tropical plants.

A path curves from the front gate past palms, ferns, and a waterfall to the house entrance. Mark hauled old ship anchor roping home from a nearby beach to use as edging along his garden path. Fifty varieties of palms, grown from cuttings, along with live oaks and coconuts shade the garden.

but when he's there, the house is wide open, with no screens—"a pass-through," he says, to the extraordinary garden outdoors. I had heard, too, about the garden, this astonishing watery jungle, how Mark had created it single-handedly out of a shabby backyard less than one-quarter acre in size. Walking through the house and out onto the deck that extends from it, I felt I had stepped into a Tarzan movie. A waterfall in the distance splashed into the large clear pool that came right up to the house, and was edged with moss-covered logs, weeping ferns, and exotic flowers. A stream led off to another pool and waterfall beyond a thatch-roofed shelter where a hammock was slung. Everywhere, the plantings were rich and jungle-like, shaded by live oaks, coconuts, and most especially, palms—queen, Washington, fishtail, princess, royal.

In the 1970s, Mark traveled down to Florida from his native Saratoga Springs, and he fell in love with palm trees and year-round warmth. He stayed and eventually started a landscape business with a friend. Twenty years ago, Mark bought his present property. "A realtor friend found this house and said you have to buy it," he recounted. "I said I couldn't afford it. She went to eleven of her friends and they signed contracts with me to do landscaping, and I got the mortgage." The house had a conventional pool in the backyard, and the first thing Mark did was rip out the concrete curbing and lattice that was its backdrop. Then he hedged the property for privacy. He grew aralia and

dracaena interwoven with fencing—chicken wire, and in some places, old shutters he salvaged and put together. "Ten months of the year," Mark says now, "you can't peer into here with a telescope."

After hedging the yard, Mark's next concern was to create shade. "I had all these tropical plants I had been growing," he says, that needed shade. "But there were no trees here." So Mark built a porch and thatched it, and then, for some fast natural shade, he planted gumbo-limbo (*Bursera simaruba*). "You can cut the trunk, put it down, and it will root," he swears. "So I covered the place with them," seven of them to be exact, three of which were lost to Hurricane Andrew in 1993.

But Mark had another problem to solve. He found his newly-shaded plants were dying when he watered them, because of the iron in his well water. "So I dug a deep hole—the limestone was soft and easy to cut through—and found fresh ground water at the bottom," he recalls. Mark decided to use a pump to bring this pure water up not only for his plants, but to create several waterfalls. PVC pipes successfully carry the water from the hole he dug to the waterfalls; from there it runs by gravity through ponds and streams he made, and finally, back to the hole.

Then he turned his attention to the swimming pool. "I was so fed up with filtering, skimming, and chemicals, that I decided

to pump this fresh ground water into it from another waterfall." He removed a piece of coping directly opposite from the waterfall so that, when the pool overflows, the water escapes there into a stream carrying with it all the flotsam, like a natural skimmer. Mark disguised the rectangular pool edges with a lip of curved, slatted decking by the house, and with mossy rocks, logs, and plants, transforming it into a pool in a jungle glade. The waterfalls operate on one pump, which costs Mark about five dollars a month to run twenty-four hours a day. Another pump draws

The back of the house opens out to decking and what was originally a traditional rectangular swimming pool when Mark bought the property. It is now fed by crystal clear spring water that Mark recirculates from a hole deep within the limestone ground, and no longer needs chemicals to keep it clean. The curved rim of the decking disguises the pool's straight edges.

The far edges of the pool are lined with mossy logs, rocks, and tropical plants. Three waterfalls, created by Mark using one pump to draw up the water deep in the ground, add to the astonishing jungle atmosphere. Mark grows all his plants from seed or cuttings, starting them in a path of compost that rims his fenced property.

water out of the pool to a sprinkler on top of the house roof to simulate a rain forest in summer. "In rainy times," Mark explains, "the plants that are growing on trees, like bromeliads, hold water; and, if I don't sprinkle they breed mosquitoes. The sprinkler virtually flushes them out and the mosquito larvae are washed away."

Having established his ingenious water systems, Mark began growing the plants to surround his pools and enclose his house in a bower of exotic foliage. Fifty varieties of palms, terrestial orchids, and all sorts of ferns, took hold and flourished. Plants I associate with indoor pot gardening and

dentists' offices—dieffenbachias and philo-dendrons, grew lustily in the gentle moisture. In 1993, however, Hurricane Andrew hit Mark's place hard. He lost almost all the palms he had grown since he moved in. "I had trees seventy-feet high. They toppled. The house was covered and crisscrossed with palm trees," which Mark thinks kept it from being destroyed. "If I'd been here," he says, on the other hand, "I'd be dead trying to save the trees."

The palms I was admiring, that recent April afternoon, were seedlings when the hurricane hit, but many of them were now forty-feet high. "The reason I have tropical

plants," Mark explains, "is that they're easy from cuttings." And, he says, there is no maintenance to speak of. "However, if we have a freeze, I'll be left with nothing." Miami is sub-tropical, Zone 11. His tropical plants would die back to the ground in a freeze, "but," he says, "they come back so fast."

"I've never bought a tree or plant," Mark tells me proudly. "They're all from seed, cuttings, and discards." He likes to call himself

The terrestial orchids, tree ferns, dieffenbachias, and palms will die to the ground if sub-tropical Miami has a frost. But these tropical plants are so quick growing that it would not take long to restore the lushness that characterizes his garden.

"a rat packer with imagination," using ingenuity to create his extraordinary garden. In a seemingly haphazard fashion, for instance, he grows cuttings and small seedlings in compost all along a working path, made with discarded newspapers, that follows the perimeters of his property. "I don't believe in fertilizer," he says. "So everything I pick up is composted. But I don't have a heap, I spread it around. I pick a spot that I want to elevate and put newspapers and junk mail down, and put vines and weeds on top, then the leaves I collect. What I take from the property, I return to the property."

Mark is justly proud of the fact that his crystal clear tropical pools contain no chemicals either. They are completely beneficial to the environment, and he claims you can drink the water. Fish ponds and waterfalls with no algae, no filtering, and no chemicals, have become his forte, and he has traveled all over Florida and in Jamaica creating them for homes as well as resort hotels. Lately, regrettably, he has stopped making these pools, because of all the red tape involved in their creation. "Now," he says, "you have to have a licensed plumber and a licensed electrician. It's no longer an art form, they've taken all the fun out of it." At a crossroads in his life, Mark is thinking of moving on in the near future, perhaps to Texas, where the same porous limestone would make it possible for him to make his naturally recycled waterfalls and ponds again.

For the time being, however, at least from November to the end of March when he doesn't landscape for people—it's too cold to install tropical gardens, he says—you can find Mark at home, swimming. "I'm a water person," he says, "I need fresh water wherever I go. I'm drawn to it." If it's ninety-five degrees outside, Mark tells me, the water and plants cool the air in and around the house to eighty-five degrees. Of course, if it's forty degrees out, it's forty degrees in the house too. But the pool is seventy-eight degrees all year round, so, "when it's forty out, the water's divine."

Frogs are Mark's nemesis. "They love it here. At night they make a noise that is deafening. It's a hell of a racket and you can't sleep. So once a month, I go frog hunting." I asked Mark if he had trouble with bugs, not having any screens. "I don't have bugs," he answered stoutly. He believes this is because he uses no chemicals, and has no lawn. "But sometimes the wind can carry mosquitoes in," he confessed. "They congregate on a mirror I have, and I vacuum them up." Spiders can take over in an open house, Mark admits, but he vacuums them up too. "House flies can be a bother sometimes in July and August. It gets a little strenuous then with the heat, so I leave town."

Not for long, however. "There is nothing so satisfying as being away, and coming back to this," Mark says. "It's just awesome that a spot could be so meaningful in your life." Does not every gardener feel this way?

Very few of us could probably live as close to the outside as Mark does, dispensing with screens and heat in the winter. But if I lived in a warm clime, I'd be tempted to have part of my house open like his, a sheltered island in a watery glade. ▪

Begonias, tradescantia, maiden-hair ferns, dwarf mondo grass, and impatiens carpet the ground of the garden.

DIMITRI STANCIOFF received a small slip of a mimosa tree in a pot as a Christmas gift from a neighbor in 1973. "It was just a little stem as thick as a pencil," he recalls. The mimosa reminded him of his childhood home in Rome, where he lived with his family in the 1930s. The driveway to their house there was lined with mimosa trees, and he remembers seeing them flowering in the snow on a chilly March day. Born in Bulgaria, Dimitri moved from there to England, and Italy, and finally to Washington, D.C., following his father's posts as a Bulgarian diplomat. Since 1967, he and his wife, Charlotte, have lived in a Victorian house in the seaside village of Camden, Maine, where he works as a marine biologist whose expertise is seaweed. Mimosas—*Acacia baileyana*—are hardy in Rome, and in the South of France, but they are not hardy in northeast Maine.

Dimitri is what I call "a dirt gardener" —someone who thrills to the actual activity of gardening, and who has the patience to watch over and wait for small plants to mature. He grows things from seed and cuttings for the pleasure of the experiment. The resulting flowers tumble riotously down his steeply-descending back yard, which he terraced over the years with stone walls, doing all the work, slowly, himself. In his vegetable garden, hundreds of tulips that he propagates from

Winter Flowering in Maine

Dimitri Stancioff's Mimosa Marvel

bulbils grow to flowering size. So, of course, he was determined to find a way of successfully cultivating his Christmas acacia.

"Mimosas are not easy to grow in a pot," he says. "They dry out easily." Dimitri decided to plant his tiny tree in the ground just outside the kitchen where the living room ell of the house on one side, and an attached barn shed on the other, gave it

Twenty years ago, Dimitri Stancioff built a glass-enclosed room outside his kitchen in Camden, Maine, to protect a small mimosa he received as a present and planted in the ground by the house wall. Today, his tender mimosa is a substantial tree, blooming racemes of yellow flowers from Thanksgiving until the end of February.

some shelter. But the tree would not survive the winter without cover. "I always wanted a greenhouse," Dimitri admits, and here was the perfect excuse—to protect the young mimosa. He built high wooden arches extending out from the kitchen, and covered them with plastic, enclosing the eleven-by-thirty-foot space between the ell and the shed. In the summer, he removed the

Dimitri salvaged the tall arched windows from an old high school in town that was being demolished, and fitted his greenhouse around them. In summer the windows are removed. Only the roof is stationary.

plastic and grew runner beans up the curved wooden ribs.

This first attempt at a greenhouse was graceful looking, he says. "But it was too flimsy, and you had to replace the plastic every year." Around 1980, the turn-of-the-century high school in town was being demolished, and Dimitri salvaged its tall arched windows to make a more substantial structure. He constructed a wooden frame, from the one wing of the house to the other, to hold the windows, then fashioned a more permanent roof with steel ribs, which he covered with transparent fiberglass. He now had an exceedingly functional cool green-house. Dimitri set up a thermostat for electric heat, which kicks in when the temperature outside hits thirty-seven degrees. Below twenty degrees, he adds a kerosene heater.

The mimosa tree thrives in this cool-ness, blooming lavishly through Maine's coldest months. Winter-flowering camellias that Dimitri grows in large pots thrive also, along with a sizeable orange tree ("it makes wonderful marmalade," he says), clivias, and a tender scented daphne. Directly in the ground just outside the kitchen door, Dimitri planted a jasmine, a fuchsia, and some tender geraniums, as well as the mimosa, where the greenhouse protects them through the winter. In the summer, he removes the series of glass windows and their frames, opening the space to sun and air. Only the Plexiglas roof is left in place. The geraniums bloom; *Fuchsia magellanica* climbs up to the roof, dangling rosy pendants; and a fragrant, starry white *Jasminum polyanthum* covers the kitchen wall. More small-flowering fuchsias and ivy geraniums hang from pipes Dimitri has strung across the greenhouse roof.

The mimosa tree is now twenty-seven years old. Its dark brown trunk is at least four inches in diameter, and its branches reach the roof and weep downward with fronds of finely-cut green leaves. From Thanksgiving until the end of February, it showers yellow flowers—shimmering racemes of crowded yellow puffs. "It grows very fast," Dimitri remarks. Each year he cuts about fifty percent of the branches out, to let air and light in, pruning in September before it flowers and then again after it blooms in March or April. Pointing out a fat nest almost hidden on one of the branches, Dimitri notes proudly that three robins were fledged there last spring.

Sitting inside the kitchen on a bitter, snowy January day, knowing many weeks of winter are still ahead, you have the thrill of glancing out the window over the sink, or opening the greenhouse door, onto this astonishing spring-like bower of lacy foliage and sunlit plumes.

"At the end of February, when the blooms begin to fade, my little granddaughter goes out to the greenhouse and shakes the mimosa tree. We call it the Rain of Gold," Dimitri says, as hundreds of gilt petals fall to the ground. ■

The mimosa tree is pruned in September before it flowers, and again in March. Half of its branches are cut to let in light and air. It flourishes in the coolness of the greenhouse, which is heated only when it dips below forty degrees.

Acknowledgments

I want particularly to thank the garden owners
and designers featured in these pages for so
generously giving their time, not to mention the
promise of meals and beds. My thanks also
go to the friends who helped me develop the book,
among them: Peggy Beal, Diane Botnick,
Dick Button, Patrick Chasse, Alice Goltra, Betsy
Hunter, Laura Palmer, Bazette Offierski,
Jane O'Neil, Dick Turner, and Anne Wilson. I am
utterly grateful to Janis Donnaud and Leslie Stoker
for their support, and to my editor, Sandy Gilbert,
for her unfailingly good-humored guidance.
Jennie Bernard cleared away cobwebs in the text,
and Susi Oberhelman skillfully combined my
words with Richard Felber's splendid pictures to
make a pleasing whole. Final thanks to my son,
Keith Dickey, and son-in-law, Don Quaintance, for
patiently talking me through each computer
crisis, and to F.J.B. Schell, my collaborator every
step of the way, who gently helped me
clarify my often vague and romantic thoughts.